*vows and suggestions of how
to pray when relationships
change or end*

Vows & Partings

The **Methodist** Church

Vows & Partings ISBN 1-85852-212-9

© Trustees for Methodist Church Purposes 2001

First published 2001

Design and production: Methodist Church Communication Office

CONTENTS

INTRODUCTION

Relationships are not static. They begin, develop, grow and change. They go through highs and lows, joys and pains. They have their significant moments, achievements and anniversaries to be marked. Some relationships come close to ending, but are rebuilt through a process of forgiveness, reconciliation, healing and restoration. Other relationships come to an end. It may be that one of the most important things that churches can do is to recognise that relationships do sometimes come to an end and people move on. A ritual to mark the end of a relationship may help, though marking the end of a marriage is likely to be a painful experience for a couple, as it is also for those close to them.

In 1998 the Methodist Conference adopted a **Report on Christian Preparation for Marriage.** Two recommendations of that Report were that 'the Family and Personal Relationships Committee, in consultation with the Faith and Order Committee, should recommend the outline of a service for the reaffirmation of marriage vows', and that 'the Family and Personal Relationships Committee, in consultation with the Faith and Order Committee and after enquiring into the resources available in other Christian communions, should explore an outline service which expresses penitence, forgiveness and new beginnings for people previously married and divorced'.

As a result, a small group was set up, with representatives from both committees. **Vows and Partings** is the result of that group's work. In line with the Report's first recommendation, it contains services for the reaffirmation of marriage vows. It does not, however, contain an outline service of the type suggested in the Report's second recommendation. This is mainly because in discussing situations in which such a service might be used, it became increasingly clear that each was so different and the needs of the individuals involved so sensitive that no one order of service would serve all situations. The needs of individuals and couples trying to find ways of expressing what is going on for them at such significant moments in their relationships are not readily met by any one order of service. So, instead, we have produced some 'suggestions of how to pray' in times of joy and pain, healing and hurt, coming together and growing apart.

The group considered whether it should seek to produce an order to mark the ending of a marriage but did not think it appropriate to produce a service releasing people from vows. Nor have we included prayers specifically relating to the bereavement and loss caused by the death of a partner or other family member because, while death is a very significant parting, there are many other resources available and it was not the focus of our task.

The variety of human experience and the complexity of people's life journeys mean we have not produced a book of easy to use 'off the shelf' liturgies. Rather, we have collected and produced some prayers and rituals and now offer them to individuals, couples, friends, ministers, pastoral carers and others as resources that might be useful.

Services for the Reaffirmation of Marriage Vows

There are churches where all the couples married over the past year, five years or ten years are invited back on a particular day to reaffirm their marriage vows. Over the past few years, some churches have begun a tradition of holding such a service during National Marriage Week (the week in February that includes the 14th, St Valentine's Day).

For some couples a church building will be the right place to mark these moments. For others it will be their own home or some other place. People sometimes choose to return to a place that has significance from an earlier time in their relationship.

We include here a complete *Service for the Reaffirmation of Marriage Vows by one or more couples.* This can be used on a special occasion in church or, where people seek a quieter, more informal, 'family' occasion, it can easily be adapted for use in the home or some other place. For those who want to mark the occasion within the regular worship of their church, we provide a *Reaffirmation of Marriage Vows for use within an act of worship.*

References to *The Marriage Service* are to *The Marriage Service* in **The Methodist Worship Book** (1999) and it is from this service that the wording for the reaffirmation of vows is taken. Couples who married using earlier orders of service may prefer to adapt the wording of the vows actually used on the day of their marriage.

Preparing a liturgy or ritual or adapting a prayer

Some significant moments in relationships are for public celebration whilst others are for private reflection with, perhaps, an individual, a couple, a few friends and close family members present. This is true for services of reaffirmation and is likely to be even more so for ways of marking other significant moments in people's relationships.

Those wanting a liturgy or ritual need to explore as clearly as possible what they are trying to do and what they want to say. For example, it may be about:
- renewing or reaffirming vows made in the past,
- marking a significant anniversary,
- confessing,
- offering forgiveness,
- giving 'permission' to move on.

This suggests that a liturgy or ritual needs to come after much pastoral care, conversation, counselling, etc. Only when the in-depth exploration has taken place should a liturgy be constructed.

A liturgy needs to be:
- sensitive to the needs of all those concerned – including those who cannot or will not be part of it,
- mutual and consensual - not forced upon anyone against their will or better judgement,
- memorable - it marks a significant step in the life of an individual, couple, family, network or community.

It also needs to be aware of the wider network of family and friends to whom a relationship is important. It may be appropriate in a service of reaffirmation of marriage vows for children or friends of the couple to take part (e.g. to place a photograph at the front of the church and say words of thanks for the gift of parents, children or friends, or for the love and affection shown by the couple to others). In such a service it is also appropriate to remember and give thanks for people who were at the original marriage service and who have since died (e.g. candles may be lit for the couple's parents and other significant people in their life and relationship).

The prayers and other material contained in **Vows and Partings** are offered as a resource, either to be used in the form printed or to be adapted to suit the needs of a particular situation.

Not just words

If the liturgy is to mark a significant, brave, perhaps painful step, silence may play an important part in the ritual.

After an informal conversation with the minister, the couple or individual may like to bring appropriate symbols from the story of their relationship. These symbols (e.g. family photos, book, candles, stones, water) may represent good times and experiences; moments of brokenness, forgiveness and healing; and/or the joy and fulfilment to which they are looking forward. A few words may be said as the symbol is put in place.

While a symbol may be helpful, care needs to be taken over what meaning will be given to it; e.g. at a marriage or in a ritual to mark the beginning of a relationship two people may use separate candles to light one larger candle. To symbolise two becoming one flesh, the separate candles may then be extinguished (they are no longer two but one). Others may prefer the separate candles to remain alight as a reminder that each individual is a person in their own right. Whichever way, the symbolism of the one candle lit from two is significant – but so is what happens to the two separate candles. The same symbol can be very effective (though painful) to symbolize the ending of a relationship, where two individual candles could be lit from one larger one and then the larger one is extinguished.

Anniversaries

A word should be said about anniversaries. Some are very public moments, and times for rejoicing and celebration (e.g. 10th, 25th, 40th, 50th, 60th wedding anniversaries). People send and receive cards and presents. Parties are held. Sometimes a prayer or liturgy is requested. It is important, even in the midst of celebration, to hold silence or to make reference to the fact that all relationships have their painful sides as well. A couple who have been married for sixty years may go through times when they wonder how they managed to survive ten!

Other anniversaries may go unmarked but be of enormous significance. Those who care for an individual may be able to share something very important by being aware of such anniversaries – the day she/he walked out on us; the last time we made love; the day the decree nisi was granted or the day the divorce 'finally came through'.

For all of us there are seasons of the heart as well as days marked on the calendar.

We hope that **Vows and Partings** will help people to bring the joys and pains of their relationships to God in worship and prayer.

David Gamble *(Convenor)*
Ann Leck
Brec Seaton
Neil Stubbens
Philip Wagstaff
Norman Wallwork *(Chair)*
Sandy Williams

January 2002

A SERVICE FOR THE REAFFIRMATION OF MARRIAGE VOWS BY ONE OR MORE COUPLES

NOTE:

When there are two or more couples, they can either make their reaffirmation at no. 13 separately, in turn, or use the alternative corporate form for several couples.

THE PREPARATION

1   The minister says:

God is love,
and those who abide in love abide in God,
and God abides in them.   *1 John 4:16*

2   Hymn

3   The minister says:

Our help is in the name of the Lord,
who made heaven and earth.
Unless the Lord builds the house,
they labour in vain who build it.
Our hope is found in Jesus Christ,
we build on him alone.

4   Let us pray

Gracious God,
you have taught us through your Son
that love is the fulfilling of the law.
In the power of your Spirit,
fill our hearts with your love
and our lives with your glory;
through Jesus Christ our Lord. **Amen**

5   The minister says:

> Those who are here today to reaffirm their marriage vows
> have gathered to seek God's continuing blessing on their life
> together.

6   Those reaffirming their vows stand.

The minister says to them:

> In God's presence
> we recall the pleasures and pains of married life
> and the years you have shared together;
> we celebrate your commitment to each other
> and the joy and strength found in your love;
> we thank God for his blessing on your lives
> and the gift of your marriage.

The minister reads from **The Marriage Service**:

> It is the will of God that, in marriage,
> husband and wife should experience
> a life-long unity of heart, body and mind;
> comfort and companionship;
> enrichment and encouragement;
> tenderness and trust.

> It is the will of God that marriage
> should be honoured as a way of life,
> in which we know the security of love and care,
> and grow towards maturity.
> Through such marriage,
> children may be nurtured,
> family life strengthened,
> and human society enriched.

Marriage involves the giving
of a man and a woman
wholeheartedly to each other.
Christ in his self-giving comes to our help,
for he loves us and gave himself for us.

The minister continues:

You have come to reaffirm your commitment
to this way of life
which God has created
and, in Christ, has blessed.
Today we pray that the Holy Spirit
will continue to guide and strengthen you
that you may fulfil God's purposes
for the rest of your lives.

THE MINISTRY OF THE WORD

7   All Sit.

At least one passage of scripture is read.

Many waters cannot quench love, neither can floods drown it.
If one offered for love all the wealth of one's house, it would
be utterly scorned.   Song of Solomon 8:7

Love is patient; love is kind; love is not envious or boastful or
arrogant or rude. It does not insist on its own way; it is not
irritable or resentful; it does not rejoice in wrongdoing, but
rejoices in the truth. It bears all things, believes all things,
hopes all things, endures all things. Love never ends.

And now faith, hope, and love abide, these three; and the
greatest of these is love.   1 Corinthians 13:4-8a, 13

As God's chosen ones, holy and beloved, clothe yourselves with compassion, kindness, humility, meekness, and patience. Bear with one another and, if anyone has a complaint against another, forgive each other; just as the Lord has forgiven you, so you also must forgive. Above all, clothe yourselves with love, which binds everything together in perfect harmony. And let the peace of Christ rule in your hearts, to which indeed you were called in the one body. And be thankful. Let the word of Christ dwell in you richly; teach and admonish one another in all wisdom; and with gratitude in your hearts sing psalms, hymns and spiritual songs to God. And whatever you do, in word or deed, do everything in the name of the Lord Jesus, giving thanks to God the Father through him. *Colossians 3:12-17*

When Jesus saw the crowds, he went up the mountain; and after he sat down, his disciples came to him. Then he began to speak, and taught them, saying:
'Blessed are the poor in spirit, for theirs is the kingdom of heaven.
'Blessed are those who mourn, for they will be comforted.
'Blessed are the meek, for they will inherit the earth.
'Blessed are those who hunger and thirst for righteousness, for they will be filled.
'Blessed are the merciful, for they will receive mercy.
'Blessed are the pure in heart, for they will see God.
'Blessed are the peacemakers, for they will be called children of God.
'Blessed are those who are persecuted for righteousness' sake, for theirs is the kingdom of heaven.' *Matthew 5:1-10*

Jesus said: 'As the Father has loved me, so I have loved you; abide in my love. If you keep my commandments, you will abide in my love, just as I have kept my Father's commandments and abide in his love. I have said these things to you so that my joy may be in you, and that your joy may be complete. This is my commandment, that you love one another as I have loved you.' John 15:9-12

Additional scripture readings are listed on page 24.

8   Readings from other sources, poems, pictures, music and memories may be shared.

9   An address may be given.

10   Hymn

THE REAFFIRMATION OF VOWS

11   The minister says:

Let us pray

Gracious God,
you brought *this couple* together in love and trust,
enable them through the power of your Holy Spirit
to reaffirm their vows;
through Jesus Christ our Lord. **Amen**

12   Those who are to reaffirm their vows stand and the minister says to them:

A and C/Husbands and wives, will you continue to love, comfort and honour each other, to be companions through all the joys and sorrows of life, and to be faithful to each other as long as you both shall live?

Answer: With God's help, I will.

13   The husband and wife turn to face each other and join hands.

EITHER (when there is one couple)

The husband says:

> *C,* on the day of our marriage
> I took you to be my wedded wife,
> for better, for worse,
> for richer, for poorer,
> in sickness and in health,
> to love and to cherish,
> from that day forward,
> until we are parted by death;
> and today I reaffirm that solemn vow.

The wife says:

> *A,* on the day of our marriage
> I took you to be my wedded husband,
> for better, for worse,
> for richer, for poorer,
> in sickness and in health,
> to love and to cherish,
> from that day forward,
> until we are parted by death;
> and today I reaffirm that solemn vow.

OR (when there are several couples)

The husbands say:

> On the day of our marriage
> I took you to be my wedded wife,
> for better, for worse,
> for richer, for poorer,
> in sickness and in health,
> to love and to cherish,

from that day forward,
until we are parted by death;
and today I reaffirm that solemn vow.

The wives say:

On the day of our marriage
I took you to be my wedded husband,
for better, for worse,
for richer, for poorer,
in sickness and in health,
to love and to cherish,
from that day forward,
until we are parted by death;
and today I reaffirm that solemn vow.

14   A hymn may be sung here or after no.15.

THE BLESSING AND THE PRAYERS

15   Those who have reaffirmed their vows may kneel and the minister says:

The blessing of God the Father,
God the Son, and God the Holy Spirit,
be upon you and remain with you always.
May God be your protection and your wisdom,
your guide and your peace,
your joy, your comfort, and your eternal rest. **Amen.**

16   Prayer of thanksgiving

The minister says:

Father of all,
we praise you for your gifts of love, joy and friendship,

for your self-giving love
shown to us in Jesus Christ;
and for the Holy Spirit
who guides us into the way of perfect love. **Amen**

Those who have reaffirmed their vows say together:

Gracious God,
we thank you for your presence in our marriage
and for the love, joy and friendship we have known.
We praise you for your guidance in times of discovery and
change,
for your comfort in times of sadness,
and for your strength in times of weakness. **Amen**.

The minister says:

God of love,
accept our thanks and praise,
in the name of Jesus Christ our Lord. **Amen**.

17   Prayers of intercession

God of grace, source of all love,
we pray for those who today
have reaffirmed their marriage vows,
that they may live together in love and faithfulness
to the end of their lives.

Lord of life,
hear us in your love.

Enrich their friendship,
that each may continue to be for the other
a companion in joy and a comforter in sorrow.

Lord of life,
hear us in your love.

Help them to be patient, gentle and forgiving,
that their marriage may reflect Christ's love for all people.

Lord of life,
hear us in your love.

Enable them to make their home
a place of welcome and friendship,
that their life together
may be a source of strength to others.

Lord of life,
hear us in your love.

May we who today celebrate your love
be signs of that same love in the world.

Lord of life,
hear us in your love.

Father of all,
we give you thanks and praise
for those who find fulfilment within marriage
and for those who find fulfilment in living alone.
We remember before you
those who now live alone
because of separation, divorce or bereavement;
and those who have never found
the relationship they longed for.

We give you thanks and praise
for all close and loving relationships

which have given meaning to our life's journey.
We remember in your presence those who have died,
and especially those who have brought us great joy.
We pray that, at the last, we may be united with them
in the fulness of your love. **Amen.**

18 The Lord's Prayer

EITHER

OR

We say together the prayer
that Jesus gave us:

As our Saviour taught his
disciples, we pray:

Our Father in heaven,
hallowed be your name,
your kingdom come,
your will be done,
on earth as in heaven.
Give us today our daily
bread.
Forgive us our sins
as we forgive those who
sin against us.
Save us from the time of
trial
and deliver us from evil.
For the kingdom, the power
and the glory are yours,
now and for ever. Amen.

Our Father, who art in
heaven,
hallowed be thy Name;
thy kingdom come;
thy will be done;
on earth as it is in heaven.
Give us this day our
daily bread.
And forgive us our
trespasses,
as we forgive those who
trespass against us.
And lead us not into
temptation;
but deliver us from evil.
For thine is the kingdom,
the power, and the
glory,
for ever and ever. Amen.

19   The Peace

      All stand.

          Jesus said:
          'As the Father has loved me, so I have loved you; abide in my
              love.'

          The peace of the Lord be always with you.
          And also with you.

      The people may greet one another in the name of Christ.

20   Hymn

FINAL BLESSING

21   The minister says to all present:

          God the Father, God the Son,
          and God the Holy Spirit,
          make *you/us* strong in faith
          and guide *you/us* in truth and love.

          EITHER   OR

          The Lord bless you   May God be gracious to us
              and keep you;   and bless us,
          the Lord make his face to   and make his face to shine
              shine on you   upon us. **Amen.**
          and be gracious to you;
          the Lord look on you with
              kindness
          and give you peace. **Amen.**

18

A REAFFIRMATION OF MARRIAGE VOWS FOR USE WITHIN AN ACT OF WORSHIP

NOTES

1   This form of *A Reaffirmation of Marriage Vows* should normally take place after the sermon.

2   If this *Reaffirmation* takes place during a celebration of Holy Communion during Ordinary Seasons, the great prayer of thanksgiving from the **Marriage Service** in the **Methodist Worship Book** may replace the one provided in the order for Holy Communion being used.

3   Prayers for those reaffirming their vows (and for their families) should be included in the prayers of intercession.

4   Though worded for use with one couple, this form can easily be adapted for use with more than one couple.

THE PREFACE

1   The persons reaffirming their marriage vows stand together before the minister, the wife on the left of her husband.

2   The minister says:

God is love,
and those who abide in love abide in God,
and God abides in them.   1 John 4:16

3   Let us pray.

Gracious God,
you have taught us through your Son
that love is the fulfilling of the law.
In the power of your Spirit,
fill our hearts with your love
and our lives with your glory;
through Jesus Christ our Lord. **Amen**

4   The minister says:

> *A* and *C*,
> you have chosen to reaffirm your marriage vows.
>
> In God's presence
> we recall the pleasures and pains of married life
> and the years you have shared together;
> we celebrate your commitment to each other
> and the joy and strength found in your love;
> we thank God for his blessing on your lives
> and the gift of your marriage.

The minister reads from **The Marriage Service**:

> It is the will of God that, in marriage,
> husband and wife should experience
> a life-long unity of heart, body and mind;
> comfort and companionship;
> enrichment and encouragement;
> tenderness and trust.
>
> It is the will of God that marriage
> should be honoured as a way of life,
> in which we know the security of love and care,
> and grow towards maturity.
> Through such marriage,
> children may be nurtured,
> family life strengthened,
> and human society enriched.
>
> Marriage involves the giving
> of a man and a woman
> wholeheartedly to each other.
> Christ in his self-giving comes to our help,
> for he loves us and gave himself for us.

The minister continues:

> *A* and *C*,
> you are now to reaffirm your commitment
> to this way of life
> which God has created
> and, in Christ, has blessed.
> Today we pray that the Holy Spirit
> will continue to guide and strengthen you
> that you may fulfil God's purposes
> for the rest of your lives.

THE REAFFIRMATION OF VOWS

5   The minister says:

> Gracious God,
> you brought *A* and *C* together in love and trust,
> enable them through the power of your Holy Spirit
> to reaffirm their vows;
> through Jesus Christ our Lord. **Amen**

6   The husband and wife face each other and join hands.

The husband says:

> *C,* on the day of our marriage
> I took you to be my wedded wife,
> for better, for worse,
> for richer, for poorer,
> in sickness and in health,
> to love and to cherish,
> from that day forward,
> until we are parted by death;
> and today I reaffirm that solemn vow.

The wife says:

> A, on the day of our marriage
> I took you to be my wedded husband,
> for better, for worse,
> for richer, for poorer,
> in sickness and in health,
> to love and to cherish,
> from that day forward,
> until we are parted by death;
> and today I reaffirm that solemn vow.

THE BLESSING

7   The husband and wife may kneel and the minister says:

> The blessing of God the Father,
> God the Son, and God the Holy Spirit,
> be upon you and remain with you always.
> May God be your protection and your wisdom,
> your guide and your peace,
> your joy, your comfort, and your eternal rest. **Amen.**

8   Prayer of thanksgiving

The minister says:

> Father of all,
> we praise you for your gifts of love, joy and friendship,
> for your self giving love
> shown to us in Jesus Christ;
> and for the Holy Spirit
> who guides us into the way of perfect love. **Amen.**

The husband and wife say together:

Gracious God,
we thank you for your presence in our marriage
and for the love, joy and friendship we have known.
We praise you for your guidance in times of discovery and
change,
for your comfort in times of sadness,
and for your strength in times of weakness. **Amen.**

The minister says:

God of love,
accept our thanks and praise,
in the name of Jesus Christ our Lord. **Amen.**

9   The service continues.

ADDITIONAL SCRIPTURE READINGS

Old Testament

Genesis 1:26-29*a*, 31*a*	Man and woman created in God's image
Genesis 2:4-9, 15-24	A husband and wife become one flesh
Song of Solomon 1:15 - 2:4	A love song
Isaiah 61:10; 62:3-5	Wedded to God

Psalms

Psalm 23	The Lord our shepherd
Psalm 121	The Lord's protection and blessing
Psalm 127 *or* 128	The gift of a family

Epistle

Romans 12:1-2, 9-13	Love in practice
Ephesians 3:14-19	Rooted and grounded in love
Ephesians 5:21-31	Husband and wife in Christian marriage
Philippians 1:9-11	Growing into a rich love
Philippians 2:1-11	The example of Jesus
1 John 3:18-24	Love in practice
1 John 4:7-12, 15-17	Love one another
Revelation 19:6-9	The wedding feast of the Lamb of God

Gospel

Matthew 7:21, 24-27	Hearing and doing
Matthew 22:35-40	The greatest commandment
John 2:1-11	Jesus at a wedding

PARTINGS AND OTHER SIGNIFICANT TIMES

The prayers and suggestions in this section are offered as ideas of how to pray in different situations. Some of the prayers could easily be used in public worship, others are much more individual and reflective in nature. The sensitivity of some of the issues dealt with means that different people will hold vastly divergent views, which are likely to be expressed in any pastoral conversation and can be reflected in how material is chosen or amended.

It may be that no prayer in this selection is appropriate for a particular situation, but it is hoped that some of the ideas may help people find ways to express what is going on for them.

CHANGING SCENES

Engagement

1   Loving God,
      we rejoice with *A* and *C*
      that they are engaged to be married.
      Bless the promises they have made;
      bless *these rings they have* given;
      and bless this time of preparation they offer to each other.
      May they come to experience
            a life-long unity of heart, body and mind;
            comfort and companionship;
            enrichment and encouragement;
            tenderness and trust.
      We offer our prayer through Jesus Christ our Lord. **Amen.**

Prayer on the occasion of an anniversary

2   Gracious God,
    we remember with thanksgiving
    the vows of love and commitment
    we made to each other in marriage.
    We pray for your continued blessing.
    In our joys and sorrows
    may we discover new riches in our life together.
    We ask this in the name of Jesus Christ our Lord. **Amen.**

Growing older, with failing health

3   Once I could run and jump,
    now my joints are stiff
    and I move with difficulty.

    Walking the dusty roads,
    Jesus taught and healed.
    He and his friends were young and active.

    Walking the roads of my youth,
    I was busy at work and at home.
    I was young and active.

    In the garden of Gethsemane
    Jesus prayed, 'Take this cup from me.'
    The cup held suffering.

    In my armchair
    I pray, 'Take this cup from me.'
    The cup holds failing health.

    In his last days Jesus was no longer active.
    People did things for him and to him.
    Mary bathed his feet, soldiers whipped him.

In my last days I am no longer active.
People do things for me and to me.
My carer bathes my body, doctors treat me.

Jesus' passion was also his time of passivity.
My old age is my time of passivity.
Yet Jesus never stopped loving.

God of compassion,
I pray that you will take away my bitterness
and as my body fails, give me a loving heart.
I ask it in Jesus' name. **Amen.**

Retirement

4   *'He makes me lie down in green pastures;*
     he leads me beside still waters;
     he restores my soul.' Psalm 23.2-3

Retirement day – the day I waited for has come and gone.
I looked forward to retirement day with anticipation,
marking the days off on the calendar.
NO MORE WORK!

Some people my age were apprehensive about retiring:
'I enjoy my job,' they would say,
'I spend time with my work-mates at lunch time,
and on Friday evenings we have a drink together.
I don't want to retire.'

Not me! I couldn't wait.
NO MORE WORK!

So much to enjoy

Why am I pacing up and down like a caged lion?
Why do I feel so discomposed and upset?
Why can't I settle to any of the tasks waiting to be done?
Why do I feel discarded and unhappy?

Loving God,
help me to make this adjustment – so much more difficult than I
    realized.
Give me a sense of purpose, a sense of worth,
and enable me to begin again.

On 'losing' a loved one to Alzheimer's

5   They say it is a living bereavement
that no one else can understand.
To 'lose' someone whilst they are still there.
Not to have the hard comfort of funeral rites.
It can be a cruel calling.

Help me to remember the 'you' that you were.
To enjoy memories that may still trigger your own fleeting
    recognition.

Help me to cherish the 'you' that is now,
still special to me even when you have forgotten why.

Help me to envision the 'you' that will one day be,
restored in the enfolding love of God,
in whom past, present and future are one,
and in whom we shall then be complete.

Lord, keep me in hope and give me strength until that day.
Amen.

                                                      Albert Jewell

WHEN TIMES ARE DIFFICULT

Relationship going through a difficult time

6   God of peace,
    we have a deep desire to live in harmony with those close to us,
    yet conflicts arise from expectations, demands, hopes and fears.
    Unite us in facing the causes of these present difficulties;
    help us to acknowledge the hurt we have inflicted on each other,
    and the pain we have had to endure;
    enable us to let go of the wrongs so that no bitterness remains
    and give us grace to forgive and receive forgiveness. **Amen.**

7   God, have you abandoned us?
    We thought that you had brought us together in love and trust;
    that Christ in his self-giving would come to our help;
    and that through the power of the Holy Spirit we would be
        enabled to keep our vows.
    We prayed that you would so join us together
    that no one would ever part us
    and that we would live together in love and faithfulness.
    Now we don't know what to believe
        about ourselves,
        about each other,
        about you.
    In our bewilderment, help us to hold on to you and to each other
    and to find in our darkness that light which cannot be
        extinguished:
    Jesus Christ, the light of the world. **Amen.**

8   God of hope,
    when every minute seems like an hour,
    when days are empty and bleak,
    when nights are lonely and long,
    when the ache inside does not fade,

help me to find peace and comfort
in the encircling of your arms. **Amen.**

Violence/abuse

9   Lord have mercy.
I never believed this could happen to me
or to one I love.

Tenderness and cruelty,
affection and abuse sometimes seem so close to one another.

Is there a living soul to listen to my story?

Where do I turn for help?
How can I find deliverance?
Is there no one who will set me free?
What in heaven's name is to become of us?

Can I ever hope to understand
or to forgive
or to forget
or to live with
all that has happened?

O Christ, bruised, broken, ill-used, pierced –
will I ever find healing in your presence?
Is it possible for you to come to me in the depths of my wounds
and journey with me into the abyss of brokenness?

Lord have mercy. Christ have mercy. Lord have mercy.

When love dies

10   Loving God,
     we feel hollow and empty
     with intentions and expectations, hopes and dreams unfulfilled:
     we had expected our love for each other to last for ever,
     that it would draw us ever-closer,
     and sustain us though bad times as well as good.
     Once it flourished, but now it has withered and died:
     like a flower of the field, it is gone.

     Forgive us that we no longer look to you
     to bless and renew us in our partnership.
     In your mercy, hear us,
     as we pray for healing and renewal in our separation.

     In the days to come,
     raise us up to new life
     in fresh relationships.

     Make us gentler in our ways
     and altogether more understanding. **Amen**

TOWARDS HEALING

Healing of hurts in relationships

11   Be with us Lord,
     when in our experience
     light turns to darkness
     and the breaking of a relationship
     leaves us stunned in our soul
     and silent in our conversation,
     not knowing where to turn or who to turn to
     or whether life has a purpose any more. **Amen.**

Reconciliation

12   Gracious God,
      you know us better than we know ourselves.
      You know our failings and all we regret.
      Help us to put away our harsh words,
      our unkind thoughts and actions.
      May we never use them
      as weapons against one another.

      As we put aside all that was hurtful and harmful
      give us the grace to forgive.
      As we gather all that is helpful and wholesome
      give us the grace to trust.

      Hands may be joined.

      And as we take one another's hands
      give us the generosity to give and receive
      wholeheartedly and with thanksgiving. **Amen.**

An act of reconciliation

13   A and B say together:

      Gracious God,
      in your presence,
      we remember the sins we have committed
      against you,
      and the wrongs we have done
      which have hurt each other.

      Silence

A says:
Holy God, holy and strong, have mercy on us.

B says:
Holy God, holy and strong, have mercy on us.

A says:
I confess to God,
Father, Son and Holy Spirit,
and also to you
that I have sinned in what I have said and done
and in what I have failed to do.

Especially, I remember and confess ...

B says:
May God who is both power and love,
forgive you and free you from your sins.
May he strengthen you by his Spirit
and raise you to new life in Christ.

Silence

B says:
I confess to God,
Father, Son and Holy Spirit,
that I have sinned in what I have said and done
and in what I have failed to do.

Especially, I remember and confess ...

A says:
May God who is both power and love,
forgive you and free you from your sins.
May he strengthen you by his Spirit
and raise you to new life in Christ.

Silence

A and B say:
The Peace of the Lord be always with you.
And also with you.

A and B may embrace each other.

Thanksgiving for new hope, after a difficult time

14   Gracious God,
we are thankful still to be together;
we could so easily be living apart.

Now we are together again
beginning to share our thoughts and feelings,
able to share a hug and a kiss,
less defensive and shuttered,
more relaxed and ready to receive love and affection.

Together
our house becomes our home,
our friends feel welcome,
and our children more secure.

When we are together
we can care for ourselves and for others.
Our relationship is not lived in isolation
and together we are whole.

Gracious God,
we could so easily be living apart;
we are thankful to be together. **Amen.**

Prayer for those wishing to renew their commitment to each other

15   Years have passed – so many days spent together:
     when the sun shone
         and the world was bright;
     when the rain poured down
         and the world was overcast;
     when we looked at each other with loving eyes,
         seeing the brightness in each other's faces;
     when we looked at each other with disappointment,
         feeling let down and disillusioned.

     Through all these days
     we have learnt to respect each other
     and to celebrate our differences.

     God of love,
     bless us as we renew our commitment to each other,
     that we may look on each other with loving eyes
     and be together in your peace. **Amen.**

SEPARATION

When someone has walked out

16   Lord Jesus,
     you know what it's like for someone close to walk out:
     you were betrayed and deserted by your friends.
     Like them, *N* has gone without a word of explanation.
     What am I to think?
     Has *she/he* gone to get away from me
     or to be with someone else?
     Will *she/he*, like Peter, deny the one *she/he* has known?
     What do I do with all these things left unresolved?
     Will we meet again?

Is there any chance of reconciliation?
Lord Jesus,
help me to know that you are with me,
and do not abandon me in my darkness. **Amen.**

Being separate

17   Lord,
there is much in my mind that has healed,
but still there is pain in my heart.
I do not always feel forgiving or forgiven:
wounds still hurt and doubts remain.

I prefer a life with no remainders
and situations with no loose ends.

Help me to understand that life is not like that.

May I find the place in my life where I can move on,
where I can be cleansed from previous bitterness,
and where I can be set free from recurring passions
    that torment my spirit. **Amen.**

Seeking forgiveness

18   God of mercy and compassion,
forgive me for the hurt I have caused to those I have loved.
Forgive the angry words, the bitter thoughts,
the resentment that wells up within me.
Forgive me when others have been caught up in our
    arguments:
friends, parents, children.
Help me to learn how to forgive as I live with my regrets.
Help me to restore relationships
with those whose trust in me has been damaged. **Amen.**

Seeking forgiveness from another person

19   God of mercy,
  give me the strength to seek the forgiveness of the one I have
    hurt.

  As I confess to them words spoken in anger,
    each one a weapon intended to wound;
  as I recall in their presence actions rooted in self-interest,
    every one a sign that the one I loved meant nothing to me;
  as I remember before them silences kept,
    preventing our frail attempts to communicate
    intentionally undermining confidence;

  God of mercy,
  give me the strength to seek the forgiveness of the one I have
    hurt.

  As I confess to them that there were better and more helpful
    ways in which to have parted;
  as I recall in their presence suffering and pain that I could have
    relieved, if I had acted differently;
  as I remember before them how I attacked them so aggressively,
    in order to defend the depth of my feelings;

  God of mercy,
  give me the strength to seek the forgiveness of the one I have
    hurt. **Amen.**

How can I begin to forgive myself?

20   Gracious God,
how can I begin to forgive myself?
Your promise is to forgive all who truly repent.
I regret what has happened and confess my part in it,
yet every day, I wake remembering –
and my guilt is a heavy weight.
Others may forgive me,
and assure me that you forgive me too,
but the dark cloud of my guilt blocks out the light of your love.

How can I begin to forgive myself?

When Jesus came face to face with Peter at the lakeside,
he asked, 'Do you love me?'
I long to hear that question and to answer
'Yes, Lord, you know that I love you,'
but my guilt is a barrier between us.

Help me to hear the voice of the risen Lord,
to accept your forgiveness,
and to forgive myself. **Amen**

Ending of a close relationship

21   Gracious God,
we remember our years together,
in which we have grown and changed.
We pray for each other as we separate.
May we be enriched by our happy memories
and let go of our painful ones.
Bless us both in our life journeys,
and give us confidence to walk into the future
strengthened by the time we have shared,
and with each other's blessing. **Amen.**

A prayer affirming the good things in a previous relationship

22 Gracious God,
   even when our hopes are left unfulfilled and our fears are
      realized,
   we know that your goodness and mercy have followed us all
      the days of our life.
   We remember before you all that was good in *A* and *C's*
      relationship:
         the happy times they shared;
         the commitment they maintained;
         the pleasures they enjoyed;
         the difficulties they overcame;
         the friends they made;
         the interests they shared;
         the home they established;
         the places they visited;
         the challenges they met;
         (the children they love;)

   For these and all your blessings to *A* and *C* we give you thanks
      and praise;
   through Jesus Christ our Lord. **Amen.**

23 Loving God,
   as I grieve for the relationship that has now ended
   help me to give thanks for all that was good
   without clinging to the past;
   help me to put aside all that was hurtful
   not allowing bitterness to cloud the present;
   above all, help me to look to the future with hope
   and believe in the possibility of a new beginning. **Amen.**

When a relationship intended to lead to marriage has ended

24   God of all goodness and source of all love,
we give you our thanks and praise
for the times of love and happiness
and the seasons of peace and contentment,
which the bonds of this friendship and companionship have
    brought.
We recall the foundations laid and the plans forged.
But now we remember before you with sorrow the days of
    darkness and difficulty that love could not sustain
and the misunderstandings that devotion could not resolve.
In your mercy forgive us
and in your love heal our hearts and memories.
Bless each of us in our separation
and, wherever we go,
keep us safe in the arms of your goodness and love;
through Jesus Christ our Lord. **Amen.**

When a marriage has ended in divorce

25   Gracious God,
we remember before you a marriage that began with high hopes.
We give you thanks for the years of joy and security
which this partnership has brought
and for the love given and received.
Now we place before you the times that have been impossible,
the hearts that have grown cold
and the feelings that cannot be resolved.
You are a God of healing and forgiveness
and we pray that bitterness may not sour our future
nor unresolved issues burn within us.
We pray that you will continue to bless and guide in separation
those who once stood before you as one.

Because none can ever fall from your caring love
keep each of us safe,
and because you alone know everything about us
heal each of our wounds.
These things we ask through our Lord and Saviour Jesus Christ.
Amen.

26　Gracious God,
you called us to live in harmony
and to reflect your perfect love;
yet despite our sincerely made promises
and all our best endeavours
we confess that we have failed you
and failed each other.
What began as we joined our lives in happiness
has ended in separation, sorrow and heartache.

We pray for those most affected
by the end of our marriage,
for our children, our family and our friends,
that they may be spared further hurt
and that we may not lose their ongoing love.
And we pray for ourselves,
that you will save us
from all resentment and bitterness,
and give us strength to rebuild our lives.

God of grace,
forgive us for what is past,
help us as we struggle with the present,
and guide us into the future;
for the sake of Jesus Christ our Lord. **Amen.**

Brian Hoare, in *And God Created Families, a Book of Prayers for Family Life.*
Family Life Committee of the World Methodist Council

27   O Lord, we pray for those who, full of confidence and love, once chose a partner for life, and are now alone after final separation. May they receive the gift of time, so that hurt and bitterness may be redeemed by healing and love, personal weakness by your strength, inner despair by the joy of knowing you and serving others; through Jesus Christ our Lord. **Amen.**   Susan Williams

A prayer for my partner at the ending of our relationship

28   God our healer,
as I pray for *N*,
I ask that you will help *her/him* at this time of change.
May *she/he* go aware that *she/he* goes with my blessing.
Help *her/him* to remember all that we enjoyed together
and to put aside unhappy and unhelpful memories.
As our special relationship ends may our friendship remain.
Amen.

Prayers for other family members affected by separation

29   Merciful God,
in disappointment and bewilderment
we turn to you.

We knew everything wasn't right,
but we never dreamt it would come to this.
Is there something more we should have said?
Something more we could have done?

Open our ears to listen to both *A* and *C,*
and our hearts to share their pain.
Help us to understand and support them
and not to rush into judgment.

Whatever the future holds,
may what we think and say and do
be filled with the love and compassion
of Jesus Christ our Lord. **Amen.**

Saying farewell, leaving people/family group

30 Lord Jesus Christ,
in Nazareth you shared the life of a family.
Then you left home,
never to return.

As we go our separate and different ways,
grant us strength of spirit
and peace of heart.

Help us to value the relationships we have made
and to treasure the experiences we have shared.

Let there be no bitterness as we move on
and no resentment as we establish our independence.

May our love for each other grow
and our enjoyment of one another flourish. **Amen.**

Giving thanks for friendship

31 Gracious God,
we thank you for the gift of our friendship
and remember the times we have shared:
    times of happiness and joy,
    of difficulty and discovery.
As we part, give us the security to move on
and to allow our relationship to enter a new phase.
Bless us both
and keep us united in the gift of your peace. **Amen.**

Loose ends

32   In the quietness I bring to God
the people who have been part of my life
but whom I do not expect to meet again;
the words I wanted to say,
but that will forever remain unspoken:
and the thoughts which I will never share.

In the quietness I bring to God
my longing
to say 'Goodbye' and to make explanations;
to thank those who have accepted and helped me;
to show those who hindered and resented me
that they bear some responsibility
for what has happened;
and to tell my side of the story.

In the quietness I listen to God's voice
encouraging me to let the loose ends remain.
Into God's keeping I place the people I love
and those I cannot remember without bitterness and resentment
welling up inside me.

In the quietness I listen to God's voice
whispering softly and insistently
that peace will come.

Leaving a house or a home

33 Lord,
this has been quite a house
in which to grow up
as parents and as children.

It has seen much laughter,
it has watched the shedding of many tears
and it has heard many an argument,
but now it is time to leave.

Help us to look back with gratitude –
to be gentle in our remembrances
and reserved in our judgments.
Let us be slow to condemn those who lived here
and lenient on its occupants
where at first we might have apportioned blame.

Thank you for the warmth of this house,
for its character,
its friendliness and, above all,
for its patience with those who once lived here. **Amen.**

NEW BEGINNINGS

A new start

34 God of mercy and new beginnings,
we remember and thank you for all that has been good in our
    past relationships
and we confess our part in all that led them to weaken and die.
As we enter a new stage in our lives,
open our hearts to receive your forgiveness,
that we may share your healing love with others.

Help us to draw on our past experiences
and come to a better understanding of ourselves
and to trust in your guidance and strength. **Amen.**

For a new sense of worth

35 God of grace, in my rejection I remember
     the cruel words which all too easily undermine my
        confidence,
     the harsh actions which make me feel worthless,
     the petty complaints which make me feel useless,
     and the scornful looks which make me feel unloved and
        unlovable.
   Help me to know that I am your child,
   of infinite worth, both loved and lovable. **Amen.**

A prayer for those entering into a new commitment

36 Blessed are you, joyful Trinity,
   Father, Son, and Holy Spirit.
   You live in the perfect unity of love.
   You have brought *A* and *C* together in friendship and love.
   Enrich their understanding and experience of each other;
   strengthen their commitment and loyalty to each other;
   and deepen their trust and joy in each other.
   Be with them in their life together
   and may they be a blessing to each other and to all they meet.
   To you be praise and glory now and for ever. **Amen.**

A subsequent marriage

The following prayers for use when either or both of those being married has been married before, may be used pastorally in marriage preparation or included near the beginning of the marriage liturgy.

37   God of the past, the present, and the future,
      we pray for *A* and *C* as they prepare
      to enter into a new marriage covenant:
      may they acknowledge their contribution
      to the strengths and weaknesses of their former *marriage(s)*;
      grow into a deeper understanding of themselves;
      and look forward to giving themselves
      wholeheartedly to each other.
      This we ask in the name of Christ
      who loves us and gave himself for us. **Amen.**

A prayer for children and young people when a parent marries again

38   It's like a whole new world,
      lots of things are different;
      but through it all,
      some things are the same.
      I'll always have my family and my friends;
      people who love me and who I love too.

      It's not my fault that things have changed!

      I'll now have two homes, and a place in each,
      which I'll make my place, with my things;
      it's exciting, but sometimes scary too.

      I've got to find out how to live at home,
      I knew how to before – but this is new.
      Sometimes I will get anxious,
      but I'll always have someone there for me.

Lord Jesus, you were a child once too.

Help me and my family to find your love;
be with me when I am anxious,
and be with me when I am happy.

Thank you for everyone who is special to me
and for all my family. **Amen.**

Prayers in a stepfamily

39   Lord,
     this is a new family.
     We have our different stories that have brought us to this place,
     but now we are bound together.

     Give us
        patience, when one of us gets things wrong;
        tolerance, when one of us talks about the way things were;
        and understanding, when we disagree because we always
           used to do things differently.

     Help us to care for each other,
     enjoy each other
     and learn to love each other. **Amen.**

PRAYERS FOR PARENTS AND GRANDPARENTS

Parenting alone

40   Those I love need so much from me –
more than I can give.
Help me, God,
when I am swamped by daily tasks,
    to find strength and patience,
    to listen to my children,
    to hear their hopes and fears,
    and to enjoy being a parent. **Amen.**

41   Jesus, people flocked to you – and you were there:
    listening, comforting,
    helping, healing,
    guiding and teaching.
Sometimes you went away to a quiet place to pray.

Jesus, my children need to know that I will listen to them;
    that when they are sad I will comfort them;
    that when they fall over, my hand will reach for the sticking
        plaster!
When I am tired and at the end of my tether,
    help me still to guide and teach them.

Jesus, when I need to get away to a quiet place where
    someone will listen to me and comfort me,
help me to find healing and guidance and strength to be a
    better parent. **Amen.**

A prayer for a parent whose son or daughter comes out

*Like many of the situations addressed in this book, this is one where people will
respond very differently and it will be important for any pastoral conversation to explore
how exactly the experience is affecting a particular parent and their son or daughter.
Any prayer said will need to be chosen and used sensitively. The following two prayers
reflect just two of many different perspectives on this issue.*

42   Lord, I do not always find it easy
to accept that my child is gay.
So many strong and harsh opinions are expressed.

Be with me in my confusion,
when the world changes,
our children defy convention
and find new ways of expressing their love.

Help us to find faith in the challenge before us
and grace to discover together the meaning of love. **Amen.**

43   Gracious God,
we need your help:
a child of our own flesh and blood claims to be gay.

We have always believed
that same sex relationships were sinful.

Lord,
we love the one you have given to us.
Help us to face this crisis together,
with firm love and with deep understanding.
Show us what to say and what to do. **Amen.**

For someone who believes they are gay

44   Father of all,
I do not fully understand the way I feel
or the way I respond to those of my own sex.

Help me to talk to other Christians
so that I can discover your will.

Show me how to be sensitive to those around me.

Be with me as I try to discern what is good, and true,
loving and appropriate. **Amen.**

A prayer to use when the next generation moves away

45   Loving Father,
I have always feared this day
and pretended, to myself, it would never come.

It is hard to watch one I love and treasure
set out to make an independent way in life.

Lord, I do not easily release my child into a harsh world,
yet, I know *she/he* cannot stay under my wing for ever.

Growth and maturity demands
a leaving of the nest and a moving on.

Overshadow us with your protecting love
and give to each of us a loving heart,
a courageous spirit
and a life filled with your peace.
May our love for you and for each other
flourish and prosper.
Lord, hear my prayer. **Amen.**

46 An empty place at the table,
     silence from the bedroom – no loud music!
     Clothes no longer strewn on the floor,
     the washing machine strangely silent.
     My child has gone away.

*'It was I who taught Ephraim to walk,
I took them up in my arms.'* Hosea 11.3

Loving God,
you are Father and Mother to your children
and you have let them go –
to grow, to live, to learn.
Your children have always made mistakes,
hurt themselves and others
and still you love them.

'How can I give you up, Ephraim?' Hosea 11.8

Loving God,
help me to let go,
to see that the house is empty
because it is the launching pad to new life.

Loving God,
help me to accept a relationship which is changing,
allowing me space
and challenging me to embrace all the possibility of a new
     beginning. **Amen.**

A prayer for a parent whose child is moving out into a new relationship

47   Lord, it doesn't seem five minutes,
      since my child was born.
      Our stories have been intertwined for so long.
      We've grown, learnt, laughed and cried together.
      As I look back,
      it's hard not to wish that things could remain the same.

      Help us to move on,
      for we have our own lives to live,
      our own stories to write.
      As *N* enters a new relationship,
      help me to know that you are always with *her/him*,
      and help us to find new ways to express our love. **Amen.**

A prayer for children at the time of divorce

48   Loving God, we pray for our children.
      At a time of change, help them to feel secure.
      At a time when memories of arguments and harsh words
        remain,
      help them to know that the arguments were ours
      and the harsh words were ours
      and ours alone;
      for our children were not the cause of our differences,
      our children were caught up in our pain and hurt by our
        mistakes.

      Loving God, we pray for our children.
      Help us to show them that they are still loved,
      by parents who will work for them and with them.
      Help us, however difficult it may be,
      to co-operate for their good;

for our children were not the cause of our differences,
our children were caught up in our pain and hurt by our
mistakes. **Amen.**

Prayers for grandparents whose grandchild moves away

49   *A candle may be lit for each grandchild*

God, the Father of us all, I bring before you *N (N and N)*
my grandchild whom I have not seen since *her/his* parents
    separated.
Our love for each other was deep and special.
I remember the fun, I remember the tears.
I remember the games, I remember the exhaustion.
I feel the loss so deeply. Help me not to be bitter.
I give you thanks for the times we shared
and the precious memories I have.
May *her/his* new home and family be stable and nurturing.
May my continuing love for *her/him* meet and join with yours;
and may *she/he* grow into adulthood with knowledge of that
    love. **Amen.**

50   Creator God, we thank you for our family.
As our children have grown we have supported them.
We have watched their children grow
and shared in their joy and pain.
Be with us in the pain that we feel
now that they have moved away.
Help us to know that even in our separation
we are held together in your love.
In all the future holds,
guide, strengthen and uphold us. **Amen.**

FINAL PRAYERS

A blessing on the journey

51   May the road rise to meet you,
     may the wind always be at your back,
     may the sun shine warm upon your face,
     the rains fall soft upon your fields;
     and, until we meet again,
     may God hold you in the palm of his hand.
     Amen.   Traditional

Lord it is night

52   Lord
     it is night.

     The night is for stillness
     Let us be still in the presence of God.

     It is night after a long day
     What has been done has been done;
     what has not been done has not been done;
     let it be.

     The night is dark.
     Let our fears of the darkness of the world and of our own lives
     rest in you.

     The night is quiet.
     Let the quietness of your peace enfold us,
     all dear to us,
     and all who have no peace.

The night heralds the dawn.

Let us look expectantly to a new day, new joys, new
possibilities.

In your name we pray. **Amen.**

The Church of the Province of New Zealand. A prayer from *Night Prayer* (p.184)
in *A New Zealand Prayer Book* (Williams Collins Publishers Ltd) 1989.
Permission sought.

INDEX

ACKNOWLEDGEMENTS

Scripture readings and scripture sentences are taken from **The New Revised Standard Version of the Bible (Anglicized Edition),** ©1989, 1995 by the Division of Christian Education of the National Council of Churches of Christ in the United States of America, and are used by permission. All rights reserved.

The text of the left hand column version of The Lord's Prayer is from **Praying Together**, © 1998 by the English Language Liturgical Commission (ELLC).

The text from the *Marriage Service* from **The Methodist Worship Book**, is used by permission of Methodist Publishing House. ©1999 Trustees for Methodist Church Purposes.